THE 7 WONDERS OF THE WORLD!

SCHOLASTIC

an imprint of
SCHOLASTIC
www.scholastic.com

Published by Tangerine Press, an imprint of
Scholastic Inc., 557 Broadway; New York, NY 10012

Scholastic Canada Ltd.
Markham, Ontario

Scholastic Australia Pty. Ltd
Gosford NSW

Scholastic New Zealand Ltd.
Greenmount, Auckland

Scholastic UK
Coventry, Warwickshire

Grolier International, Inc
Bangkok, Thailand

10 9 8 7 6 5 4 3 2 1

ISBN-10: 0-545-05470-2

ISBN-13: 978-0-545-05470-6

Made in China

THE 7 WONDERS OF THE WORLD

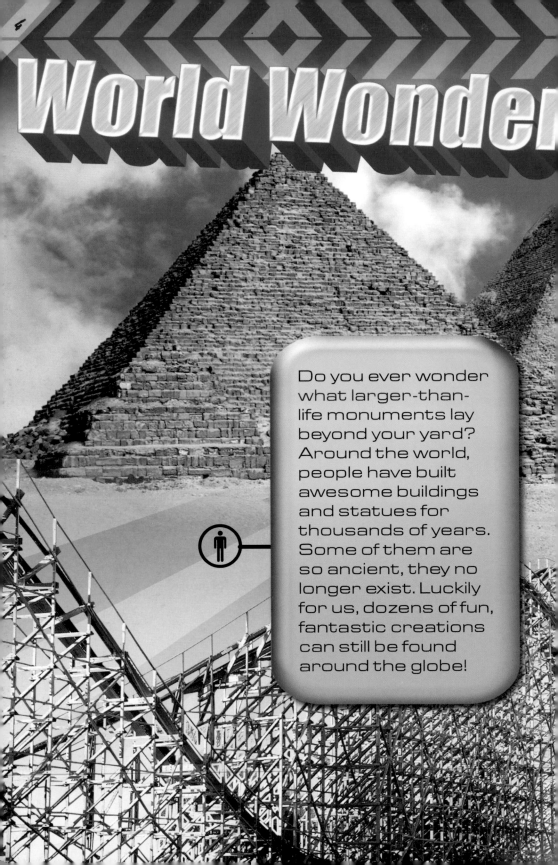

World Wonder

Do you ever wonder what larger-than-life monuments lay beyond your yard? Around the world, people have built awesome buildings and statues for thousands of years. Some of them are so ancient, they no longer exist. Luckily for us, dozens of fun, fantastic creations can still be found around the globe!

PAST AND PRESENT

From way-cool roller coasters to a colosseum, a waterfall to the longest wall, an indoor beach to an Australian reef, Earth is home to many exciting places. So, grab your passport and a camera, because your adventure is about to begin!

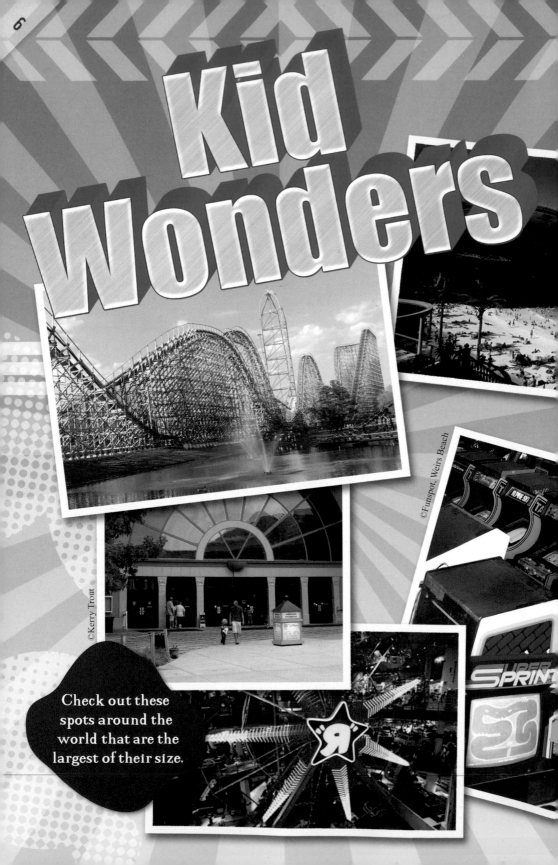

Kid Wonders

©Funspot, Weirs Beach

©Kerry Trout

Check out these spots around the world that are the largest of their size.

World wonders don't just include high mountains, deep canyons, or great walls. Some of the biggest, best places may be right in your own neighborhood! Check out the largest toy store and video arcade, and find out where to go if you want to climb the world's biggest tree house or swim in the biggest water park. If you have a fear of roller coasters or *T-rexes*, take caution!

©Convic

1. CEDAR POINT
Sandusky, Ohio; U.S.

2. THE CHILDREN'S MUSEUM OF INDIANAPOLIS
Indianapolis, Indiana; U.S.

3. TOYS "Я" US TIMES SQUARE
New York City, New York; U.S.

Where in the World?

1.

2.

3.

4.

Kid Wonders

4. FUNSPOT
Weirs Beach,
New
Hampshire; U.S.

5. THE ALNWICK
GARDEN
TREEHOUSE
Alnwick,
England

6. SMP SKATE
PARK
Shanghai,
China

7. OCEAN
DOME
Miyazaki,
Japan

THE BEST

AMUSEMENT PARK

STATS

LOCATION: Sandusky, Ohio; U.S.

SIZE: 364 acres (147 ha)

HIGHLIGHTS: Top Thrill Dragster, Millenium Force, and Raptor roller coaster

CEDAR POINT

If you love amusement parks, you just have to check out Cedar Point, the largest in the world! It has 68 rides, from roller coasters to waterways and Krazy Kars to carousels. This gigantic park opened in 1870, making it the second-oldest park in the U.S.

DID YOU KNOW?

Wicked Twister is the tallest and fastest "double twisting" impulse roller coaster ever made. It is U-shaped and reaches 215 feet (65.5 m) into the air!

Daredevils can brave topsy-turvy, ultra-fast thrill rides like Demon Drop and Chaos. Or take a whirl around the world! Circular and spinning rides like the Matterhorn or Super Himalaya will prove to be a super-swirly treat.

Cedar Point has 17 roller coasters, more than any other park on Earth. It also has Top Thrill Dragster, one of the tallest roller coasters in the world at 420 feet (128 m), and races at 120 mph (193 kph)! Altogether, you'll find 47,353 feet (14.3 km) of coaster tracks throughout this park just waiting to be conquered.

CHILDREN'S MUSEUM

DID YOU KNOW?

The Children's Museum of Indianapolis houses three dinosaurs—a Mastodon, an *Ankylosaurus,* and a life-size *Tyrannosaurus rex!*

©Kerry Trout

STATS

LOCATION:	Indianapolis, Indiana; U.S.
SIZE:	433,500 square feet (40,272 m²)
HIGHLIGHTS:	Three dinosaurs, a polar bear, an Indianapolis 500 race car, and a mummy's tomb

THE CHILDREN'S MUSEUM OF INDIANAPOLIS

How would you like it if you had a garden with your very own *Ankylosaurus*? At The Children's Museum of Indianapolis, an outdoor exhibit has just that—perfect for climbing!

This museum of monstrous proportions is definitely the biggest children's museum in the world! It has three dinosaurs, a 19th-century locomotive, 11 galleries, and more than 100,000 artifacts. Every year, more than a million people of all ages visit this six-story attraction.

But the best part is that while most museums are hands-off, that's not the case here! You can dig for dino bones, excavate a mummy's tomb, explore an underwater coral reef, walk through a haunted house, and watch the wonders of the starry universe in the planetarium.

It's also filled with artwork from around the globe. Drawings, paintings, and sculptures are some of the types of art you'll find scattered throughout this enormous museum! After a long day of exploring, you may be inspired to make your own artwork—maybe someday, it will be shown in an awesome place like this!

THE BEST

TOY STORE

STATS

LOCATION: New York City, New York; U.S.

SIZE: 110,000 square feet (10,219 m²)

HIGHLIGHTS: Ferris Wheel, Candy Land shop, lifesize Barbie® Dollhouse, *Jurassic Park* exhibit, LEGO® shop

TOYS "Я" US TIMES SQUARE

In New York City, New York, what would you expect to find among the hustle and bustle of everyday life? How about a five-ton (4.54-tonne) *Tyrannosaurus rex*, or a 25-foot-tall (7.6-m) Empire State Building made of LEGO® bricks?

At Toys "Я" Us Times Square, that's exactly what you'll find, along with many other outrageous toys and contraptions. Since November 2001, this three-story store has welcomed toy lovers from around the world.

On the 60-foot (18.2-m) Ferris Wheel, climb into a cab themed by a different toy, television, or movie character, including E.T., Mr. Potato Head, and Buzz Lightyear. Come face to face with a 20-foot-tall (6-m), 34-foot-long (10.3-m) *T-rex* that roars to life in the Jurassic Park® Exhibit. If you've ever wanted to go inside a real-life dollhouse, the two-story, 4,000-square-foot (371.6 m²) Barbie® Dollhouse is a dream come true. This toy store also has special rooms for magic shows, playing musical instruments, and making your own stuffed animals, too!

THE BEST

ARCADE

©Funspot, Weirs Beach

STATS

LOCATION:	Weirs Beach, New Hampshire; U.S.
SIZE:	60,000 square feet (5,574 m²)
HIGHLIGHTS:	500 new and classic arcade games, annual Classic Video Game contest

FUNSPOT

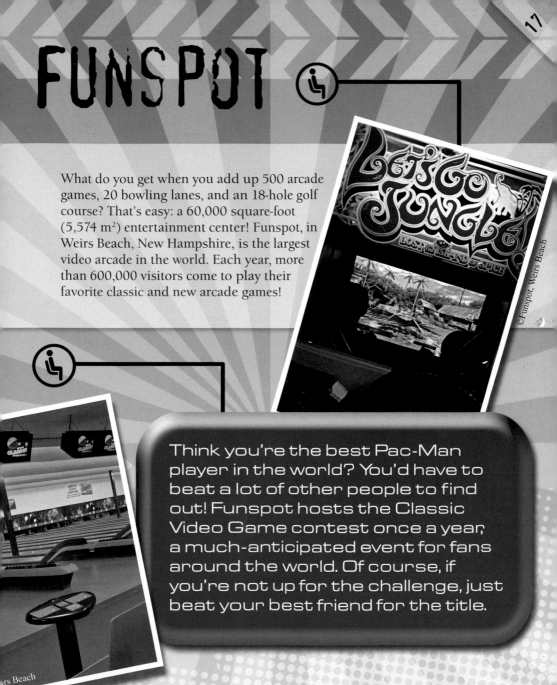

What do you get when you add up 500 arcade games, 20 bowling lanes, and an 18-hole golf course? That's easy: a 60,000 square-foot (5,574 m²) entertainment center! Funspot, in Weirs Beach, New Hampshire, is the largest video arcade in the world. Each year, more than 600,000 visitors come to play their favorite classic and new arcade games!

©Funspot, Weirs Beach

Think you're the best Pac-Man player in the world? You'd have to beat a lot of other people to find out! Funspot hosts the Classic Video Game contest once a year, a much-anticipated event for fans around the world. Of course, if you're not up for the challenge, just beat your best friend for the title.

Once you've had your fill of the arcade games, bowling, and mini-golf, you're still not done! Firework spectacles, haunted houses, bingo games, and car shows are some of the other festivities you'll find at Funspot. So, save up those coins and be ready to get your game on!

THE BEST

TREE HOUSE

STATS

LOCATION: Alnwick, England
SIZE: 6,000 square feet (557.4 m²)
HIGHLIGHTS: Aerial ramps and walkways, tree-trimmed cottages, a cozy restaurant with a fireplace

THE ALNWICK GARDEN TREEHOUSE

Have you ever wondered what kind of zany things you would do if you had your own tree house? Do you think you'd eat dinner in it, sit by its fireplace, or wobble across its bridge? Maybe these don't sound like things you'd do in your dream tree house, but that's exactly what happens right in Alnwick Gardens—home of the biggest tree house in the world!

Opened in 2005, the 6,000-square-foot (557.4-m²) tree house is made up of cottages linked by bridges, ramps, and walkways. If you enjoy being suspended over a forest floor and a ravine, surrounded by squirrels and swaying branches, you'll feel right at home!

DID YOU KNOW?

Besides a tree house, the Alnwick Garden has a maze and a safe garden full of poisonous plants!

The Duchess of Northumberland dreamed up and created the tree house as a charity program. It cost almost $7 million (£3.3 million) to build. It is specially designed to welcome disabled people, with its ramps and wide, wooden walkways. She wanted to build a "safely dangerous" space for curious adventurers of all ages who are eager to play, exercise, learn, and relax in a fun, elegant setting.

THE BEST

SKATE PARK

©Convic

STATS

LOCATION: Shanghai, China
SIZE: 147,000 square feet (13,656 m²)
HIGHLIGHTS: Mondo Bowl, competition areas

SMP SKATE PARK

How would it feel to be shot up into the air from a 17-foot (5.2–m) vertical ramp? Skaters from around the world find that out at the SMP Skate Park in Shanghai, China. Dubbed the world's largest skate park at 147,000 square feet (13,656 m²), this park of colossal proportions has world-class ramps, bowls, and street courses.

Competitors from around the globe trek to SMP every year. While SMP provides a challenge for professional skater showdowns, it has more than enough space for beginner practice.

DID YOU KNOW?

SMP's famous Mondo Bowl has a 66-foot-long (20-m) full pipe and a 164-foot-wide (50-m) vert ramp.

Some of this skate park's bowls are as low as five feet (1.5 m), while others skyrocket to more than 15 feet (4.6 m) high. So no matter where you venture in this epic-sized park, you're sure to become airborne!

WATER PARK

STATS

LOCATION:	Miyazaki, Japan
SiZE:	322,920 square feet (30,00 m²)
HiGHLIGHTS:	Indoor beachside ocean, Mount Bali Hai volcano, Lost World rain forest

OCEAN DOME

Whip out your beach towel, suntan lotion, and sunglasses for a trip to Ocean Dome, the world's largest indoor beach and ocean! Even on a rainy night, you can soak up the Sun. Ocean Dome is the world's largest indoor water park.

This ocean is completely artificial, from its salt-free water to its plastic rain forest. You can even hear the computerized parrots chirping from the treetops. Every hour, a fake volcano erupts, and it billows smoke every 15 minutes. When fake flames burst out, water pumps create incredible waves. Surf's up!

DID YOU KNOW?

In this domed paradise, the overhead roof opens and closes to let in real sunlight, but the temperature is always 86°F (30°C).

Three thrilling water slides surround the volcano. A train chugs through the Lost World rain forest, where spooky, holographic ghosts, sea pirates, and Jurassic dinosaurs prowl after you. This amazing indoor beach is open 365 days a year.

Natural Wonders

Pack your snorkel and hiking boots for this next wild adventure: we're going back to nature! Natural wonders can't be created by humans, but are formed by Earth's weather and forces. These natural beauties will continue to change slowly over thousands of years as Nature takes its course.

CNN made this really cool list of seven natural wonders.

1. NORTHERN LIGHTS
Northern Hemisphere

2. GRAND CANYON
Arizona, U.S.

3. PARICUTIN VOLCANO
Michoacán, Mexico

Where in the World?

1.

2.

3.

4.

Natural Wonders

4. HARBOR AT RIO DE JANEIRO
Rio de Janeiro, Brazil

5. VICTORIA FALLS
Zambia and Zimbabwe

6. MOUNT EVEREST
Nepal and Tibet

7. GREAT BARRIER REEF
Australia

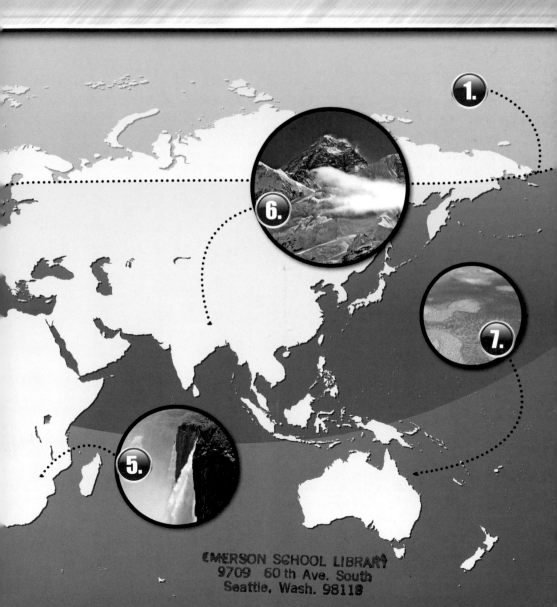

LOCATION: Northern Hemisphere
SIZE: 50-150 miles (80-241 km) above the earth
HIGHLIGHTS: Shades of light arch over the night sky, sparking mystery, awe, and the human imagination.

NORTHERN LIGHTS

Imagine having a light show in your own backyard, one that drapes over the night sky in brilliant shades of blue, violet, green, and red! This phenomenon—known as the aurora borealis—has been described in mystical myths and legends for centuries.

DID YOU KNOW?

You may see lights in the Southern Hemisphere, too! The aurora australis occurs in the Southern Hemisphere, but it's not considered a wonder of the natural world.

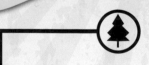

Until science could explain these lights, stories of their existence were passed down in many cultures. Inuits, who live in the northern polar region, tell of spirits who travel along the night sky with torches, lit by the flames of the aurora borealis. In Medieval times, Europeans claimed the lights were omens or heavenly warriors. This spectacle gets its name from two ancient words: Aurora, the Roman goddess of the dawn, and Boreas, the Greek name for the north wind.

This light show begins as a dim glow on the horizon, and rises into a dramatic arc over the night sky. When particles of a solar wind collide and interact with Earth's magnetic field, the energy they create becomes light.

GOTTA SEE

STATS

LOCATION: Arizona, United States

SIZE: 1,462,560 feet (446 km) long

HIGHLIGHTS: Deep-cut gorges, sky-scraping plateaus, and trickling tributaries make up the Grand Canyon.

GRAND CANYON

Did you ever think rainwater could make a lasting impact on giant, unmovable rocks? At one point, peaks that would have rivaled the world's tallest mountain range (the Himalayas) may have stood in Arizona. Now, nearly 1.7 billion years later, this long-gone mountain range makes way for an American natural wonder, mostly because of rain, flash floods, and the Colorado River.

Although no one knows for sure how the Grand Canyon formed, there are many educated guesses. Erosion probably played a large part: the desertlike ground can't absorb water, so it rushes with rocks and soil to the nearby Colorado River. Like a snowball in an avalanche, the water's volume and speed increases until it becomes a flash flood! Over millions of years, erosion continued to carve the canyon's crevices.

DID YOU KNOW?

Limestone, granite, shale, and sandstone make the rusty-red rocks of the canyon seem to glow from miles away— even from an airplane!

Nine hundred years ago, Pueblo people named the Anasazi lived in the Grand Canyon. In 1540, the first European, a Spanish explorer, found this wonder while searching for a legendary city of gold. While the Canyon doesn't hold golden treasures, it definitely is a treasure to see!

STATS

LOCATION: Michoacán, Mexico

SIZE: 1,390 feet (424 m) tall

HIGHLIGHTS: This newly-formed volcano was the first ever to be studied from its first eruption to its last.

PARICUTIN VOLCANO

Just imagine: during a hard day's work plowing your corn field, loud hissing noises rise from the earth. The soil shakes, the land splits, and stones and soot shoot into the air. The ground swells into a cinder-cone shape, and an eruption occurs, spewing lava onto the land! Farmer Dionisio Pulido, his wife, and son witnessed just this—the birth of Mexico's Paricutin Volcano in 1943.

Many geologists (scientists who study the earth's structure) came to learn about this modern marvel. For the first time ever, they were able to research a volcano through its entire life cycle. That's because in 1952, the lava flowed from the Paricutin Volcano for the final time. Although it would never erupt again, Paracutin left the world with a better understanding of volcanoes' life cycles and unstoppable power.

This natural wonder stands out for one main reason: The modern world had never witnessed the formation of a volcano before. Within its first year, it grew to almost full-size. It erupted frequently, but the volcano's lava trickled very slowly. Families in Paricutin and nearby villages had to move, because after two years, these areas were almost completely buried under lava.

STATS

LOCATION: Rio de Janeiro, Brazil

SIZE: Approximately 342 square miles (886 km²)

HIGHLIGHTS: Hundreds of islands and mountains surround this beautiful bay.

HARBOR AT RIO DE JANEIRO

In January of 1502, Portuguese explorers sailed up a narrow coastline where the Atlantic Ocean meets the Guanabara Bay. Coming closer to the coast, they found green hillsides, peaking crags, and beautiful mountains around the mouth of a large inlet. Thinking this site led to a river, they named the body of water after the month they found it: the Rio de Janeiro, or the "River of January."

Wild animals like jaguars and tapirs once roamed this tropical coast. Today, the land has highways, an art museum, beaches, parks, and an airport. Famous for its tourism and local landmarks, Rio de Janeiro's harbor may be overcrowded and polluted, but its awe-inspiring skyline is something to see.

In 1555, the French founded the first colony in the area of Rio de Janeiro. Nearby, the Portuguese settled, too; they used their newly-formed city to build a fort against the French! Nearly ten years later, the Portuguese drove the French out of the settlement.

DID YOU KNOW?

Pirates frequently attacked the harbor. In 1711 French pirate René Duguay-Trouin sacked the city for two months.

GOTTA SEE

STATS

LOCATION: Zambia and Zimbabwe

SIZE: 328-351 feet (100-107 m) tall

HIGHLIGHTS: Tourists can raft, kayak, canoe, and fish on the water's wild rapids, with wildlife, such as hippos and crocodiles.

VICTORIA FALLS

DID YOU KNOW?

You can see Victoria Falls by helicopter, horseback, or bungee jumping from a nearby bridge.

If you lived in Zambia, Africa, and someone asked you, "What's the name of that waterfall?" you might answer, "Mosi-oa-Tunya!" The Kololo tribe gave it this name, which means "The Smoke that Thunders." In 1855, Scottish explorer David Livingstone came upon this natural wonder and renamed it Victoria Falls for British Queen Victoria.

Two parks preserve the peace and wildlife of Victoria Falls—Mosi-oa-Tunya National Park in Zambia and Victoria National Park in Zimbabwe. These parks are home to some of the world's most well-known animals, including giraffes, elephants, zebras, and lions.

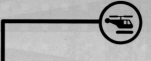

The countries of Zambia and Zimbabwe are separated by a 328-foot-(100-m) deep split that forms Victoria Falls. From above, it seems as if the earth has been cracked. Water from the Zambezi River rushes down at incredible speeds, spraying water hundreds of feet into the air.

STATS

LOCATION: Nepal and Tibet

SIZE: 29,035 feet (8.8 km) tall

HIGHLIGHTS: Mount Everest is so mythical yet dangerous that people have risked their lives climbing its perilous peaks.

MOUNT EVEREST

Satellite View

If you were to climb more than 29,000 feet (8.8 m) up the world's highest mountain, Everest, how long do you think you'd chill out at the top? Two days? Twelve hours? Thrill seekers who trek up this treacherous mountain usually stay there for...half an hour! Worrying about freezing darkness, afternoon weather storms, or limited oxygen supply means that climbing up—and down—Mount Everest is all in the timing.

In 1953, Edmund Hillary and Tenzing Norgay were the first to reach Mount Everest's peak using oxygen tanks. Brave climbers must face freezing-cold winds, shifting ice blocks, and avalanches to survive. Only about 2,000 people have made it all the way to the top. Many climbers pay locals to help them; these expert guides are called "sherpas."

DID YOU KNOW?

For families who want to brave Mount Everest without risking their lives, Disney's Animal Kingdom has a 112-foot (34-m) roller coaster called "Expedition Everest" that has snowlike peaks.

This glorious mountain rises right on the border of Nepal and Tibet. Nearly 60 million years ago, India had been its own continent and collided with Asia. The force of the land masses caused the earth to swell upward, forming what is now Earth's highest mountain.

STATS

LOCATION: Australia
SIZE: 1,243 miles (2,000 km) long
HIGHLIGHTS: Marine life, from shellfish to great white sharks, humpback whales to dolphins, sea turtles to sea snakes.

GREAT BARRIER REEF

DID YOU KNOW?

The Great Barrier Reef is so large that it can be seen from outer space!

The word's largest and most fragile natural wonder is the Great Barrier Reef in Australia. This reef contains many different animals and plants that depend on it for food and shelter. Many researchers, wildlife lovers, and scuba divers come here each year to enjoy the reef's beautiful scenery and unique creatures.

The Great Barrier Reef Marine Park protects part of this reef because of dangers from the environment. Pollution caused by chemicals, copper deposits, humans' litter, and oil spills harm the area. Overfishing and climate changes are also harming the reef. Some animals, like loggerhead turtles, are endangered, which means that they may die off. They need special protection in order to survive.

The Great Barrier Reef is an underwater treasure, but not just the kind that holds gems, gold, or shipwrecks: it has exotic, colorful marine life, 900 islands, and nearly 3,000 reefs. It's made up of colonies of dried polyps (tube-like creatures with a mouth and tentacles) rooted to the sea floor.

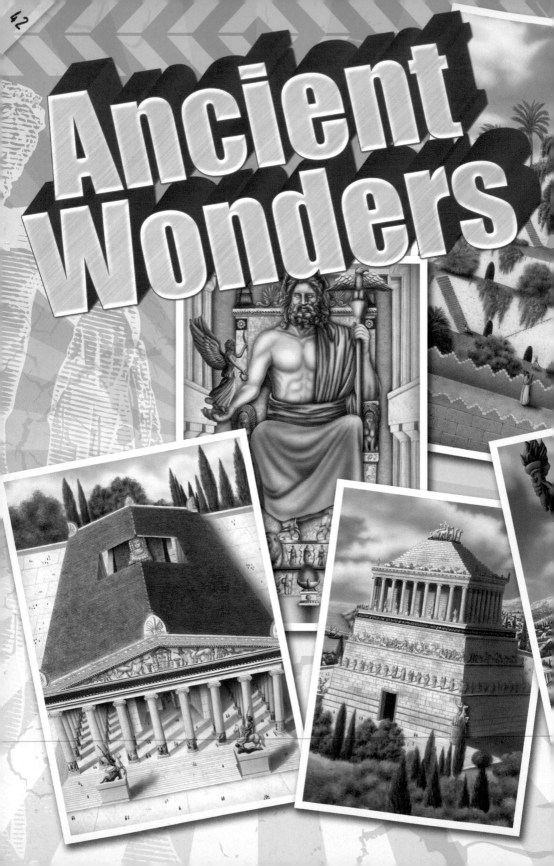

Ancient Wonders

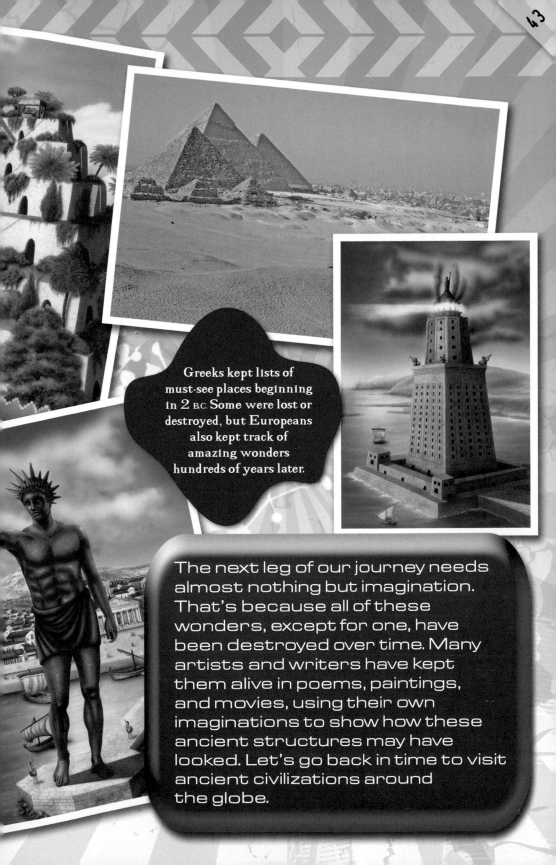

Greeks kept lists of must-see places beginning in 2 B.C. Some were lost or destroyed, but Europeans also kept track of amazing wonders hundreds of years later.

The next leg of our journey needs almost nothing but imagination. That's because all of these wonders, except for one, have been destroyed over time. Many artists and writers have kept them alive in poems, paintings, and movies, using their own imaginations to show how these ancient structures may have looked. Let's go back in time to visit ancient civilizations around the globe.

1. STATUE OF ZEUS AT OLYMPIA
Olympia, Greece

2. TEMPLE OF ARTEMIS AT EPHESUS
Ephesus, Turkey

3. MAUSOLEUM AT HALICARNASSUS
Bodrum/Halicarnassus, Turkey

Where in the World?

Ancient Wonders

4. COLOSSUS OF RHODES
Rhodes, Greece

5. LIGHTHOUSE OF ALEXANDRIA
Pharos/ Alexandria, Egypt

6. GREAT PYRAMID OF GIZA
Giza/ Cairo, Egypt

7. HANGING GARDENS OF BABYLON
River Euphrates or Baghdad, Iraq

STATS

LOCATION: Olympia, Greece

SIZE: Approximately 37–40 feet (11–12 m) tall

HIGHLIGHTS: Made of thousands of precious stones, ivory panels, gold plates, and ebony pieces.

STATUE OF ZEUS AT OLYMPIA

The Greeks built a temple around 450 B.C. to honor Zeus, the Greek god of justice. The temple seemed too simple for such a supreme god, so a sculptor named Phidias made a statue of Zeus. It was so tall, it reached the ceiling. Had it come to life, Zeus' head would have gone right through the roof!

This king of the gods had ivory skin and a gold robe. He held a staff in his left hand and the goddess of victory in his right. Mythological scenes decorated Zeus's throne, which contained many jewels. Greek athletes gathered at Zeus' shrine beginning around 776 B.C. They competed in contests every four years. These athletic games were eventually called the Olympics, named after the city where they began.

In the 4th century A.D., the worship of pagan gods was banned. The Olympics came to an end, and the great statue of Zeus was moved to Constantinople, Turkey. The original temple of Zeus in Olympia was burned to the ground, and later, in A.D. 462, the statue of Zeus was also lost in a fire. The modern-day Olympics would be revived—but all that remains of Zeus' statue are the historic writings of its eyewitnesses.

CHECK IT OUT

STATS

LOCATION: Ephesus, Turkey

SIZE: Approximately 111,800 square feet (10,386 m²)

HIGHLIGHTS: The temple was also used as a banking and trade center. It drew visitors from as far as India and Persia.

TEMPLE OF ARTEMIS AT EPHESUS

With the hope that his name would never be forgotten, a madman named Herostratus set fire to one of the most amazing world wonders in 356 B.C.—the Temple of Artemis at Ephesus. Although much is known about Herostratus, the same can't be said about the Greek goddess' lost temple.

Foundations for the building were laid in the 7th century B.C., but the temple as we know it was built around 550 B.C. Two rows of 60-foot (18–m) columns—127 in total—rose around the temple. Known as "the great marble temple," its interior was filled with gold and silver sculptures. They were created by the finest artists at the time—including Phidias, designer of Zeus' statue in Olympia!

Greeks rebuilt Artemis' temple several times, but they, too, were destroyed. The only hints we have of the temple's appearance come from early detailed descriptions. Eventually, archaeologists (scientists who study past cultures) found remains 20 feet (6.1 m) below muddy soil. Researchers still continue to dig for clues, hoping to piece together what they can of this lost marvel.

STATS

LOCATION: Bodrum/Halicarnassus, Turkey

SIZE: Approximately 135 feet (41 m) tall

HIGHLIGHTS: This building had unique statues and a structure that mixed Greek, Persian, and Egyptian styles.

MAUSOLEUM AT HALICARNASSUS

Mount Everest, Braille, the Dewey Decimal system, and bloomers are all named after well-known people. The Mausoleum at Halicarnassus was also named after someone. When Persian King Mausolus died in 353 B.C., his body was laid to rest in a gigantic tomb. Although this world wonder fell to ruins, monumental tombs would be forever known as "mausoleums."

Queen Artemisia loved her husband, King Mausolus, so much that she had a monument built for him. It was 135 feet (41 m) high, with three levels. The top level was a pyramid-shaped roof that seemed like a staircase rising into the sky. Underneath, a boxy core held the roof's weight, surrounded by 36 slim, Greek-style columns. The bottom level was the tomb itself, a podium made mostly of marble, with dozens of sculptures around the platform.

For 16 centuries, the grand mausoleum withstood the test of time—until an earthquake damaged it during the 1400s. Knights used the rubble to build fortresses, and sections of the marble tomb can still be found in nearby castle walls today.

STATS

LOCATION: Rhodes, Greece

SIZE: 110 feet (33.5 m) tall

HIGHLIGHTS: This statue has come to represent freedom and unity.

COLOSSUS OF RHODES

The Greek island of Rhodes, also the name of its capital, was a flourishing region. Rivals tried to invade the city, but they couldn't take it over. They left their bronze military equipment in Rhodes. Legends say the Rhodians melted down the weapons to build this statue of Helios, the sun god, to honor and thank him for their wealth and good fortune.

DID YOU KNOW?

The Colossus survived only 56 years, shorter than any other wonder. It was destroyed by an earthquake.

A monumental statue stands at the entrance of a harbor; its outstretched arm bears light, overseeing ships and welcoming visitors. The Statue of Liberty is not an ancient world wonder—but she was inspired by this Greek original nearly 1,600 years earlier!

No one really knows what this statue looked like. Throughout time, many artists imagined how Helios may have appeared: standing with a foot on either side of the inlet or feet firmly together; raising a torch above his head or carrying a bow and arrow. The mystery of this wonder now lives on in art, poetry, and films.

STATS

LOCATION: Pharos/Alexandria, Egypt

SIZE: Approximately 384 feet (117 m) tall

HIGHLIGHTS: The Lighthouse of Alexandria was the first lighthouse of its kind in the world.

LIGHTHOUSE OF ALEXANDRIA

With the island of Pharos nearby, the city of Alexandria's coastline created dangerous sailing conditions for ships. Alexandria, named for Alexander the Great, was a busy city full of knowledge, trade, and culture. The only world wonders that functioned—the Pharos Lighthouse—was built for the safety of seafarers.

The lighthouse, nicknamed "Pharos," was the last of the now-extinct world wonders to disappear. After earthquakes destroyed it, Egyptians used its broken stones and timbers to build a fort where the Pharos once stood.

We know of the lighthouse's appearance for two main reasons. An Arab traveler wrote a detailed description of the building in the 1100s. Alexandrian coins also showed a picture of the Pharos—much like many coins today feature national monuments! The Pharos had three levels, each a different shape: a lower-level square, a middle octagon, and an upper cylinder. The building's peak held a statue of Poseidon, the sea god who ensured safe passage for sailors.

DID YOU KNOW?

Lighthouses around the world earned their names from the Pharos. "Faro" (Spanish and Italian), "phare" (French), and "farol" (Portuguese) all mean "lighthouse."

CHECK IT OUT

STATS

LOCATION:	Giza/Cairo, Egypt
SIZE:	451 feet (137 m) tall
HIGHLIGHTS:	With its unshakable structure, The Great Pyramid has withstood the tests of time.

GREAT PYRAMID OF GIZA

Although three pyramids stand together on the West Bank of the Nile River, only one is a world wonder. This pyramid, called the Great Pyramid, was built as a burial place for the pharaoh Khufu. When he died, Egyptians carefully mummified his body and sealed him in a stone tomb for eternity.

According to an ancient Arab proverb, "Man fears Time, yet Time fears the Pyramid." That's because the Great Pyramid of Giza, the oldest of the world wonders, still stands today! Amazingly, it took 20 to 30 years to build, with the help of many architects, engineers, peasants, and farmers.

DID YOU KNOW?

The Great Pyramid was Earth's tallest structure until the Lincoln Cathedral was finished in the 1300s.

There may be more than 2,300,000 stones that make up this structure! Once, the exterior of the pyramid was covered in a sparkling limestone, which made it shimmer. Its interiors are filled with hallways, escape shafts, and galleries, and in the center of it all is the pharaoh's burial chamber. Even though the tomb was robbed of its treasures, the Great Pyramid still stands.

STATS

LOCATION: River Euphrates or Baghdad, Iraq

SIZE: Approximately 400 square feet (37.2 m²)

HIGHLIGHTS: These gardens may have had exotic plants and flowers, a pool, and beautiful terraces.

HANGING GARDENS OF BABYLON

How many legends can you name that seem like they existed, but no one can prove for sure? Some examples might include Atlantis, Camelot, the fountain of youth, or El Dorado. The Hanging Gardens of Babylon is the only world wonder that may well be a made-up tale, but people have been looking for it for centuries.

Ancient historians described this mysterious wonder in their writings, the only way we know about its possible existence. The kingdom of Babylon did actually exist, under the rule of King Nebuchadnezzar II. Legend has it that when his wife became homesick, the King built this mountainous garden for her.

There is a chance that another ruler may have built the Gardens, although the King was famous for building beautiful palaces, temples, and roads throughout Babylon. Poets have described the garden-structure as having a pool with running streams, overhanging plants and flowers, stairways, columns, and tree-lined terraces.

The New 7 Wonders

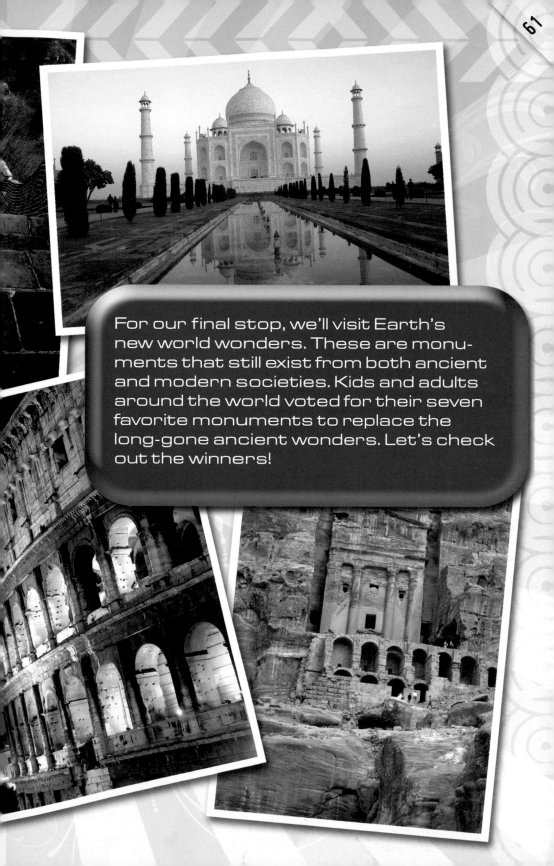

For our final stop, we'll visit Earth's new world wonders. These are monuments that still exist from both ancient and modern societies. Kids and adults around the world voted for their seven favorite monuments to replace the long-gone ancient wonders. Let's check out the winners!

1. CHICHÉN ITZÁ
Between Cancun and Merida, Mexico

2. MACHU PICCHU
Machu Picchu district, Peru

3. CHRIST THE REDEEMER
Rio de Janeiro, Brazil

Where in the World?

The New 7 Wonders

4. ROMAN COLOSSEUM
Rome,
Italy

5. PETRA
Petra,
Jordan

6. TAJ MAHAL
Agra,
India

7. GREAT WALL OF CHINA
Liaoning to
Gansu,
China

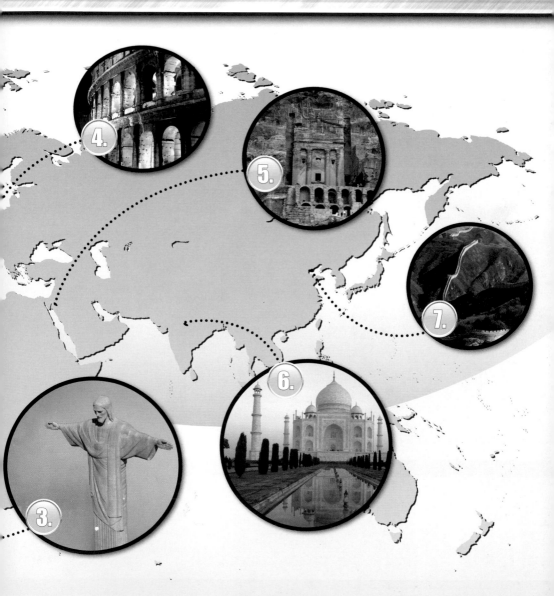

The New 7 Wonders
The New Seven Wonders The New Seven Wonders The New Seven Wonders Th...

STATS

LOCATION: Between Cancun and Merida, Mexico
SIZE: 4-6 square miles (10.4-15.5 km^2)
HIGHLIGHTS: The Great Ball Court, the Pyramid of Kukulcan, cenote

CHICHÉN ITZÁ

Chichén Itzá, an ancient, sacred site, was occupied and influenced by many different people from A.D. 1 to 1441, notably the Mayans. In the 8th century, seafaring, merchant warriors conquered and settled in this area, near a cenote, Spanish for "well." This cenote held much-needed water for the land, and the city became famous for its religious, economic, and political power.

Chichén Itzá holds many architectural marvels, including the Great Ball Court. Two teams played on this gigantic court—40 feet (12.2 m) long—using only their hips, elbows, or wrists to hit balls through stone hoops on the court's walls. Only the most honorable were chosen to play.

The Pyramid of Kukulcan, where ceremonies were held, most likely relates to astronomy. Twice a year, the Sun's position over the pyramid creates a long shadow down these steps that looks like a giant, slithering snake heading toward the sacred cenote. This ancient city still represents many religious and social mysteries, which archaeologists hope to one day uncover.

The New 7 Wonders

STATS

LOCATION:	Machu Picchu district, Peru
SIZE:	5 square miles (13 km^2)
HIGHLIGHTS:	Well-preserved palaces, temples, baths, parks, and houses

MACHU PICCHU

In 1911, Peruvian locals led an American archaeologist named Hiram Bingham to a spectacle "hidden" atop a 9,000-foot- (2.7-km) high mountain—the ruins of mighty Machu Picchu. The Incas once lived in this city built of stones. Hidden by clouds, it's like an oasis on the mountaintop. "Machu Picchu" means "Old Peak" in Quechua, a Native American language.

DID YOU KNOW?

Located only 2,000 miles (3,219 km) above a rumbling river, Machu Picchu is also known as "The Lost City of the Incas." Built in the 1400s, it is nearly invisible from the valley below, as surrounding jungles and clouds hide it from sight. Palaces, parks, temples, homes, and farming terraces reveal the ruins of a once-rich community.

Machu Picchu's walls are pieced together with heavy stone blocks. They fit together so tightly that not even a sharp blade can pierce the crevices.

The Incas abandoned Machu Picchu in 1573. They may have left because they didn't want to be conquered by Spanish explorers. Even though the Spaniards came close, they never found Machu Picchu.

The New 7 Wonders

STATS

LOCATION:	Rio de Janeiro, Brazil
SIZE:	130 feet (39.6 m) tall
HIGHLIGHTS:	A durable, welcoming religious icon

CHRIST THE REDEEMER

On a mountain peak overlooking Brazil's Rio de Janeiro, a huge statue stands with wide, open arms. Since the mid-1800s, several statues were proposed to serve as a landmark for this largely Catholic city. In 1921, a monument was finally agreed on: a statue of Christ standing in the shape of a cross.

Construction on the statue lasted five years—from 1926 to 1931—and was finally made public on October 12, 1931. Designed and sculpted by a local Brazilian engineer and a French sculptor, the statue weighs 700 tons (635 tonnes) and stands 130 feet (40 m) tall. It is made of reinforced concrete and soapstone. This religious marvel is a welcoming sight to tourists and locals.

Christ the Redeemer stands at the summit of Corcovado Mountain in Tijuca Forest National Park. Visitors can reach the statue by train, which leads to elevators, escalators, and a stairway of exactly 222 steps. At the statue's base is a chapel, where weddings and baptisms are traditionally held.

STATS

LOCATION: Rome, Italy

SIZE: Approximately 160 feet high, 615 feet long, 510 feet wide (49 m x 187 m x 155 m)

HIGHLIGHTS: Entertainment arena, gladiator battles

ROMAN COLOSSEUM

The Colosseum was the place to be if you were a Roman citizen. Audiences watched battle re-enactments, classical dramas, mock sea battles, animal hunts, and, of course, gladiator fights. For nearly 400 years, the Colosseum hosted epic gladiator battles.

The Colosseum looks like today's football stadiums. Because the entire floor was covered in sand, Italians called it an arena. In Latin, arena means "sand." When it became too sunny, a large awning could even be pulled overhead. Due to earthquakes and robbers, two thirds of the original building is missing, although the Colosseum continues to stand as a wonder of Roman architecture.

DID YOU KNOW?

Almost 50,000 spectators could be seated in the marble chairs, but surprisingly, it only took five minutes for the entire audience to clear out!

The New Seven Wonders The New Seven Wonders The New Seven Wonders The New Seven Wonders T...

The New
7
Wonders

STATS

LOCATION:	Petra, Jordan
SIZE:	30 square miles (77 km²)
HIGHLIGHTS:	The Treasury, the Theater, royal tombs

PETRA

On a trade route for merchants of Israel, Lebanon, and Saudi Arabia, a secret entryway leads through narrow gorges beyond towering cliffs to the rocky city of Petra, Jordan. Hidden in the desert, Petra existed for about 400 years, but no one knows exactly when or why it was built.

This city made of mountains survived in the scorching desert thanks to manmade dams and waterways, which collected water for thirsty residents. After winding through a secret tunnel, spectators come upon the Treasury, a monument of columns and statues carved straight out of the mountainside. Depending on the time of day, the sandstone rock appears different colors— from pink and mauve to yellow, gray, and white.

New trade routes were introduced by Roman rulers around A.D. 100. This sign of a changing world led to Petra's downfall. Earthquakes destroyed several of its buildings in A.D. 363, as well as its vital water systems.

The New 7 Wonders

LOCATION: Agra, India

SIZE: 144 feet (44 m) tall

HIGHLIGHTS: Beautiful decorations, white marble walls, onion-shaped dome, royal tomb

TAJ MAHAL

Emperor Shah Jahan was so saddened by his wife's death that he created a memorial for her. It's a mausoleum made of white marble, named the Taj Mahal. This monument was built in 22 years by 20,000 workers. It's the final resting place of both the emperor and Queen Mumatz Mahal.

The Taj Mahal was built by Muslim rulers of India, called the Mughals. Plant and flower designs, gemstones, geometric shapes, and Arabic calligraphy (a decorative style of handwriting) were carved and painted on nearly every surface of the building.

DID YOU KNOW?

The Taj Mahal's most striking feature is its onion- or lotus-shaped dome. Lotuses are India's national flowers, and often stand for purity of heart and mind.

The Taj Mahal is made up of the mausoleum, the main gate, the mosque, the garden, and the rest house. In the garden, a long rectangular pool reflects the Taj Mahal and the overhead sky. Many people come here to find peace.

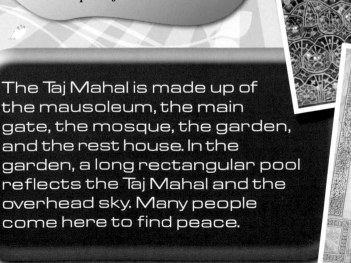

The New Seven Wonders The New Seven Wonders The New Seven Wonders T
The New 7 Wonders

STATS

LOCATION: Liaoning to Gansu, China

SIZE: Approximately 4,163 miles (6,700 km) long

HIGHLIGHTS: Ancient walls, able to ward off invaders, more than 2,000 years old

GREAT WALL OF CHINA

Like a legendary Chinese dragon snaking over mountains, deserts, and grasslands, the Great Wall of China winds from East to West across the country. However, this wonder—the longest manmade structure ever built—spans more than land: it spans thousands of years of Chinese dynasties, invasions, and rulers.

In 770 B.C., the Zhou Dynasty began construction of the wall to keep out northern invaders. At first, it was divided into smaller walls, which kept Mongolian tribes out of Chinese states. The separate walls were joined together around 220 B.C., creating a unified China at last.

DID YOU KNOW?

Each dynasty contributed to the Great Wall in its own way. In Beijing, a section of the wall is made of blue bricks, which rise to an average height of 26 feet (8 m).

Castles, fortresses, and watch-towers also make up the Great Wall. It was originally made from grass, wood, stone, and earth, but to build a better defense, bricks and granite were later used. Cannons were eventually added, and armies were posted, ready to warn of an invasion at a moment's notice.

WHAT'S YOUR WONDER?

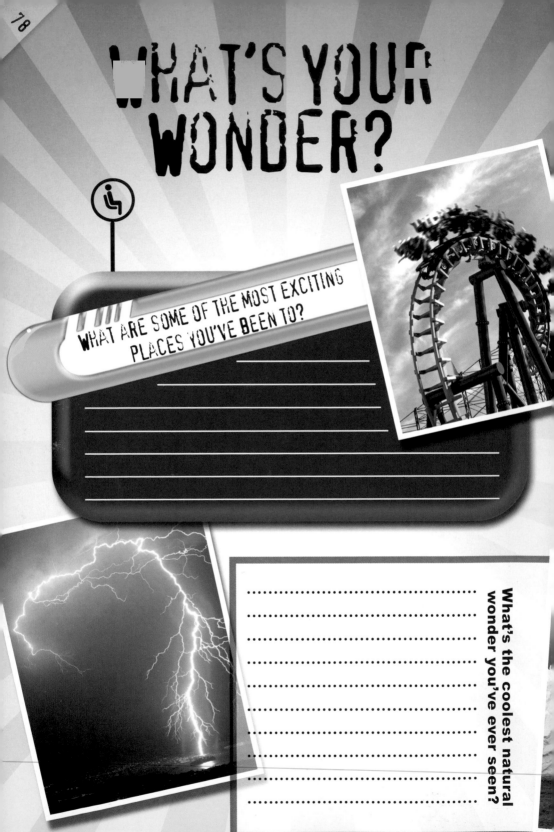

WHAT ARE SOME OF THE MOST EXCITING PLACES YOU'VE BEEN TO?

What's the coolest natural wonder you've ever seen?

What places would you name as world wonders?

_____

_____

_____

_____

1.

2.

3.

4.

5.

6.

7.

IF YOU COULD MAKE YOUR OWN WORLD WONDERS, WHAT WOULD THEY BE?

IT'S A WONDERFUL WORLD

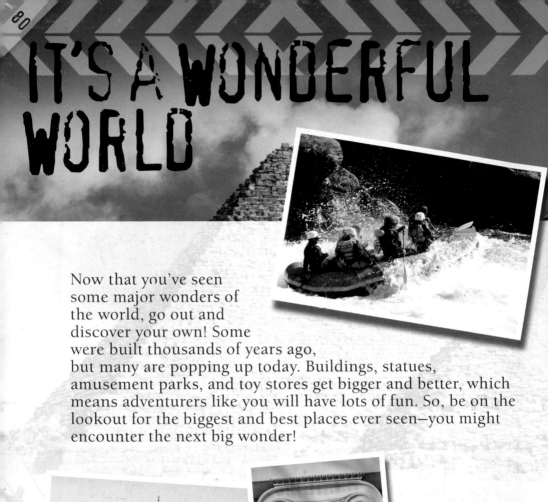

Now that you've seen some major wonders of the world, go out and discover your own! Some were built thousands of years ago, but many are popping up today. Buildings, statues, amusement parks, and toy stores get bigger and better, which means adventurers like you will have lots of fun. So, be on the lookout for the biggest and best places ever seen—you might encounter the next big wonder!